The American Negro

THE
AMERICAN
NEGRO

A Study in
Racial Crossing

by

MELVILLE J. HERSKOVITS

GREENWOOD PRESS, PUBLISHERS
WESTPORT, CONNECTICUT

Library of Congress Cataloging in Publication Data

Herskovits, Melville J. (Melville Jean), 1895-1963.
　　The American Negro : a study in racial crossing.

　　Reprint. Originally published: New York :
Knopf, 1928.
　　Bibliography: p.
　　Includes index.
　　1. Afro-Americans--Anthropometry.　I. Title.
GN57.A35H47　1985　　　　　573'.6'08996073　　　85-7671
ISBN 0-313-24795-1 (lib. bdg. : alk. paper)

Copyright 1928 by Alfred A. Knopf, Inc.

Reprinted with the permission of Alfred A. Knopf, Inc.

Reprinted in 1985 by Greenwood Press
A division of Congressional Information Service, Inc.
88 Post Road West, Westport, Connecticut 06881

Printed in the United States of America

10 9 8 7 6 5 4 3 2 1

For My Father

Preface

FOR the student of human biology, the gathering of the data on which his conclusions are based presents a serious problem. Unlike the geneticist, who works with non-human forms of animal life, the anthropologist has little control over the selection of his material. He must trust to the good-will of the people among whom he is working, to their understanding and willingness to coöperate with him in his research, and to the chance of the moment. We of this day pride ourselves on our acceptance of the methods of science, and on our realization of the desirability of scientific research. Yet when a study touches man, the prejudices and superstitions that lie deep in our cultural heritage come to the fore, and too often we are not willing to submit.

The results set forth in the following chapters represent research conducted over a period of four years. During those years I measured some thousands of persons, and my assistants have measured more. Anthropometric research, if it is to be successful, must be coöperative, and consequently I have accumulated many debts of gratitude to persons who have helped, financially and otherwise, in mak-

Preface

ing this study possible. It is a pleasure to make my acknowledgments at this time to some of those who have assisted me in the undertaking.

The major portion of my research was accomplished as a result of an appointment which I received from the Board of Fellowships in the Biological Sciences of the National Research Council, which allowed me to devote three years to this problem. The Columbia University Council for Research in the Social Sciences, at the instance of Professor Franz Boas, allotted funds to me for indispensable assistance, and allowed me a fourth year in which to analyze the material gathered during the preceding three. The Committee on Human Migrations of the National Research Council, through Dr. Clark Wissler, appropriated funds which permitted greater latitude in my work at Howard University. To my assistants, Mr. Louis King, Mr. Abram L. Harris, Miss Zora Hurston, and Mr. Greene C. Maxwell; to Dr. Jacob M. Ross, principal of Public School 89 and later of Junior High School 139, New York City, and to his teaching staffs in these two schools; to the President and Faculty of Howard University, and particularly to Professors Ernest E. Just and Alain L. Locke; and to Miss Beatrice Blackwood and Frau von Luschan, I wish to express my gratitude for numerous favors, loyal coöperation, and patient forbearance. The

Preface

interest and guidance of Professor Franz Boas, at whose suggestion I undertook this research, have been a constant source of inspiration to me, and it is with deep pleasure that I acknowledge my indebtedness to him. Finally, I may say that without the graciousness of the people whose measurements go to make up this study, without their coöperation when they would have been entirely justified in withholding it, my research could not have proceeded.

To all of these I am privileged to express my gratitude. To them is due whatever of value this bit of research may hold. Its shortcomings, however, are my own.

MELVILLE J. HERSKOVITS

Evanston, Illinois
October 22, 1927

Contents

INTRODUCTION
page xiii

CHAPTER I
The Amalgam He Represents
page 3

CHAPTER II
The Physical Type He Is Forming
page 18

CHAPTER III
The Description of His Physical Type
page 34

CHAPTER IV
White Values for Colored Americans
page 51

Contents

CHAPTER V

His Significance for the Study of Race
page 67

BIBLIOGRAPHIC APPENDIX
page 83

INDEX
page 89

Introduction

WHEN in 1619—as John Rolfe tells us in John Smith's *Generall Historie*—there came "a Dutch man of warre, that sold us twenty Negars," the Negro problem, in all likelihood, was first introduced into what was to become the United States of America. For some three hundred years since then, these Africans and their descendants have lived among us. What has happened to them in that time? What contacts have they made? To what extent have they mingled their blood with that of the other peoples of this country? What have they given their neighbors, and what have they taken from them? How have they influenced them, and been influenced by them? I know of no more fascinating problem, nor of one which has been more inadequately dealt with. Our knowledge of the African ancestry of the American Negroes is of the vaguest. We know that they were exported from the Guinea Coast of West Africa; but we can only guess from how far inland they came. The stages of acculturation through which they passed after their arrival in this country have never been adequately described, nor, so far as one can see, are they likely

Introduction

to be. Even to the casual observer, however, it is obvious that Negroes have become an integral part of our civilization. They have solved the problem of meeting its requirements, though in a manner that may sometimes seem heightened and exotic. But what has happened to them as individuals is not so obvious. We must investigate what changes, if any, have taken place in their physical form and in their mental processes, before we can understand them. In the following discussion I present the results of an extended investigation of the physical form of the American Negro, and endeavor to throw some new light on the problems which have arisen concerning him.

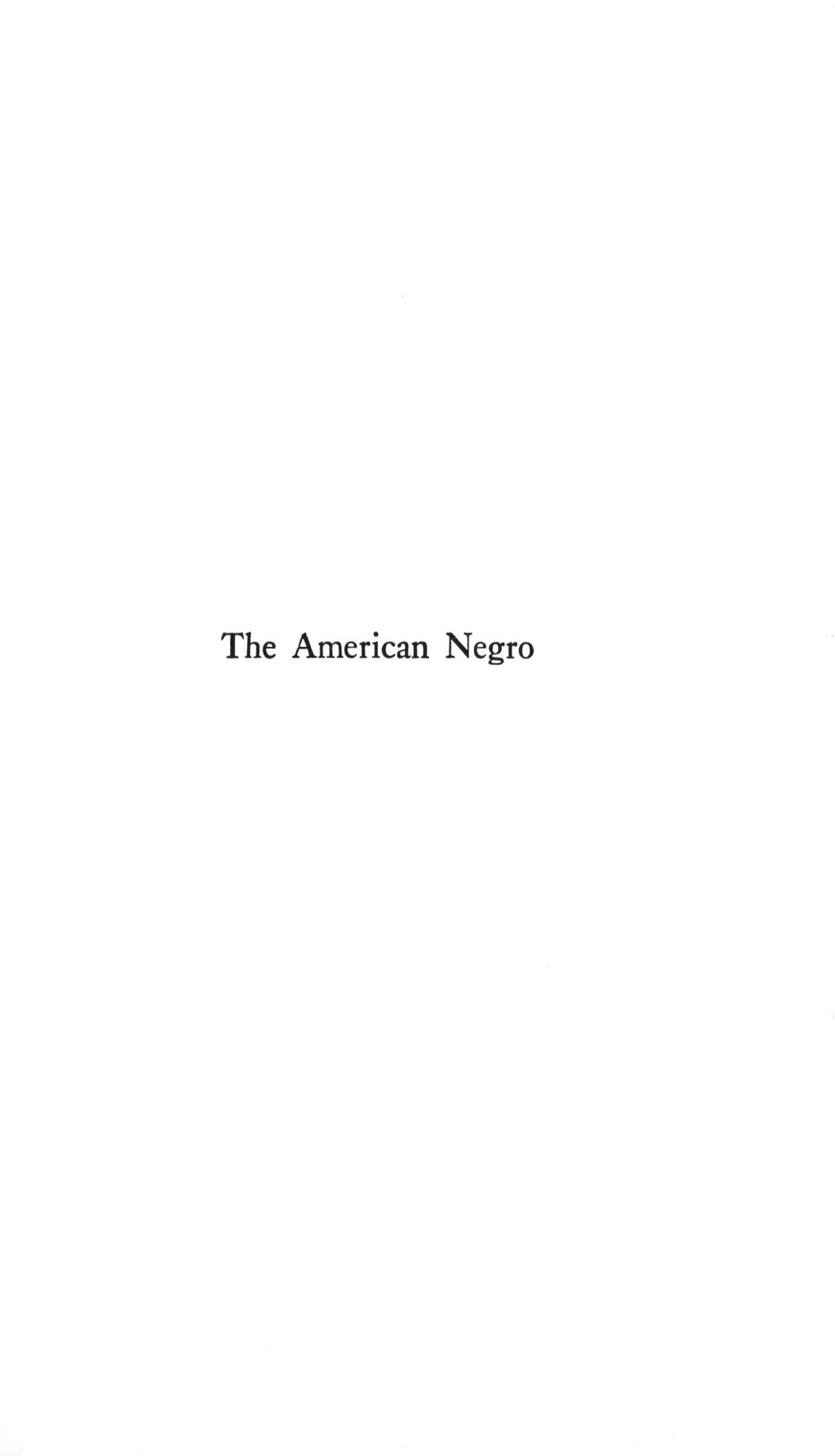

The American Negro

I

The Amalgam He Represents

THE phenomenon of race crossing seems to hold endless fascination for students of population, of race, of genetics—indeed, for students of all phases of human development. A maxim which is never challenged in fact—since the fact is self-evident—is that two human groups never meet but they mingle their blood. It is this fact that makes the position of the American Negro peculiarly valuable for biology. Because the Negroes were slaves, the law of the masters was paramount; and the masters, as in all slave lands, took the slave women for themselves. But the offspring of a slave was also a slave, and so the mixed-bloods were regarded as "Negroes," while the White stock remained largely free from the introduction of Negro blood.

Furthermore, there were American Indian peoples throughout the Southeast in the early days, and with these the Negroes mingled to a degree that Whites usually fail to recognize, though to a Negro knowledge of Indian ancestry is a matter of pride. This mingling also took place in the West Indian Islands,

The American Negro

whence came many of those who later formed part of the American Negro community. Thus to the Negro-White mixture a third element was added, so that in the American Negro of today we find represented the three principal racial stocks of the world: Negro ancestry from Africa, Caucasian from northern and western Europe, and Mongoloid (American Indian) from southeastern North America and the Caribbean Islands.

Obviously we have here an approximation to laboratory conditions for studying the results of human mixture, for we are dealing not only with a crossing of two races, but with a mingling of the three principal racial stocks! How has this crossing affected the bodily form of the Negroes? Are they Africans? Have the Negroid traits predominated? Or have the component ancestral traits mingled in the physical form of these people? To what extent, indeed, are these ancestral elements present in the contemporary American Negro population? For this is the first problem we must attack. In stating that this African population has undergone extensive crossing with other racial groups during its residence in the United States I should make clear that I am advancing a postulate which is far from universally accepted. The census figures of 1920 state that there are 10,463,131 Negroes in this country. Of these, we are informed, 8,802,577

The Amalgam He Represents

are "Black"—that is, unmixed Negro, or, to quote the instructions issued to the enumerators, "Negroes of full blood." On the other hand, only 1,660,554 Negroes are listed as "Mulatto" or, again quoting, as "Negroes having some proportion of White blood." In other words, in 1920 it would appear that 84.1 per cent of our Negroes were of pure blood, while only the remaining 15.9 per cent were mixed. It is interesting to remark that the proportion of "Mulattoes" reported to the census-takers has decreased since 1910, when 20.9 per cent of the Negroes listed were so classified.

Although there are reasons for suspecting the reliability of these figures, they have been accepted by most scholars because of the absence of detailed investigation into the ancestry of the American Negro. It is usually stated that the vast majority of Negroes in the "Black Belt" are unmixed Africans, but that those in the North represent a considerable amount of White ancestry. This argument has given rise, in turn, to an untenable assumption frequently encountered in discussions of the American Negro. Professor Jerome Dowd, for example, in his recent work on the Negro problem, strongly emphasizes a two-fold division of the Negro population: on the one hand, a small, active, violently discontented and agitating Mulatto group; and on the other, a large, sluggish, socially immovable, more or

The American Negro

less shiftless and irresponsible unmixed-Negro group. Professor Reuter, in his well-known book on the Mulatto, also utilizes the official estimates for the number of mixed Negroes when he considers the relative social position of the two supposedly socially distinct groups. In his recent study, however, he questions the government figures. Dr. Mecklin is another sociologist who has discussed the Negro problem with an eye to this division. The Mulatto, he tells us, is "a *Zwischending* ethnologically and socially," temperamentally discontented with his inferior position, and unwilling to identify himself with the lowly full-blood with whom he is grouped in the minds of the dominant Whites.

Because of the general belief that the "pure" Negroes were in the great majority, I at once found it essential to face this problem and to devise a method for obtaining information regarding the amount of mixture represented by the American Negro. To what extent is he a child of Africa, groping his way about a White civilization? To what extent may he claim a place in the culture of this country by partial blood-right, as well as by virtue of the contributions of his two hands? It was no easy matter to secure this information. How was one to obtain a control with which to check the figures commonly accepted by students of the Negro problem? Obviously, if control were to be exercised,

The Amalgam He Represents

the method of looking at a Negro and classifying him as mixed-blood or unmixed Negro, which is that utilized by the census enumerators, would be unsound. My study was primarily an anthropometric one, concerned with the measurement of certain definite physical traits—traits in which there are distinct differences between Africans and Europeans. But reliance on these measurements alone, in view of the scantiness of our knowledge of the manner in which human traits are inherited, seemed only slightly more desirable than dependence on the rough and ready methods of the census. One method remained—a simple one, but one which had been discarded *prima facie* by students who had considered the problem. This was the genealogical method—that of merely asking the people measured about their descent.

The objections to this method are familiar to everyone; indeed, they are stock jokes among Whites, many of whom assert that the sexual looseness of Negro women is such that "the Negro doesn't know who his father is." From this plane the theory goes through various gradations, until it reaches a culmination in the refusal of many of the life insurance companies to insure Negroes on the partial ground that, not knowing their ancestry with reliability, Negroes cannot declare diseases which may possibly be hereditary in their families. The

The American Negro

few companies which insure Negroes increase the premium rates for them, again with this reason prominently given. In spite of this argument—and so often is it reiterated that it gains strength even in the minds of the skeptical—I determined to gather genealogies among the adult Negroes I measured. This was made possible when I worked first at Howard University, and later when work was done among the Harlem population of New York City, and still later in a rural community in West Virginia.

Let us examine the results of these studies, disregarding, for the moment, the question of the reliability of the genealogies obtained, the question of the reliability of all Negro genealogical material, and the question of the extent to which the Negro, may or may not know his father. First, however, we must point out how the individuals were placed in the several genealogical classes. This I did as conservatively as I was able to do it. A given individual was classified only on the basis of the actual information given by him. If he stated that, to the best of his knowledge, three grand-parents were unmixed Negro, and if he had no information at all about the fourth grand-parent, then he was classified as unmixed Negro. If he knew of one White grand-parent and of another who was mixed Negro-White, and knew nothing of the other two, he was classi-

The Amalgam He Represents

fied as more White than Negro. In this way eight classes were formed, as will be noted. Four of these represent differing degrees of Negro blood, and there are four corresponding classes for the subjects who were aware of some Indian admixture. The amount of Indian blood, however, is not indicated, since mixture with Indians is not a thing of the recent past. The classifications of the statements given by adult male and female Negroes who were measured were tabulated, and in the following table are given the classes, the number of individuals represented in each, and the percentage of the total number represented by each class:

Class	Number of Individuals	Percent of Total
Unmixed Negro	342	22.0%
Negro, mixed with Indian	97	6.3%
More Negro than White	384	24.8%
More Negro than White, with Indian	106	6.9%
About the same amount of Negro and White	260	16.7%
The same class, with Indian mixture	133	8.5%
More White than Negro	154	9.3%
More White than Negro, with Indian	75	5.5%
Total	1551	100.0%

The American Negro

This story differs somewhat from that found in the usual estimates of the amount of crossing. Here we have the astonishing information that, instead of 80 or 85 per cent of the American Negroes being wholly African in descent, only a little over 20 per cent are unmixed, while almost 80 per cent show mixture with White or American Indian, or with both stocks. Furthermore, this table points to another conclusion of importance in a consideration of the American Negro's physical form and ancestral background. This is the fact that, according to the statements of the Negroes measured in this study, between one-third and one-fourth of them (27.3 per cent, to be exact) have American Indian ancestry, although the reliability of this percentage cannot be controlled by any method with which I am familiar.

At this point the problem of the validity of the genealogical information obtained in this study comes to the fore. These statements and figures contradict the accepted statistics so strikingly, that commentators are certain to raise the obvious objection, namely, that the men and women who gave these genealogies were ignorant of their family histories. But, as I have said, the data gathered include a large number of physical measurements of the persons involved. Indeed, these measurements were the primary object of this research; the genealogies were a by-product, an experiment undertaken

The Amalgam He Represents

on the chance that this sort of information, in spite of everything that had been maintained, might throw some new light on the problem. But when the tabulated results showed such startling percentages, it was clear that an attempt to control their validity should be made. The physical measurements furnish this control. For, as will be understood by anyone who has ever had any contact with Negroes (unmixed Negroes, that is), the physical differences between these individuals and either Whites or Indians are striking. The differences between Whites and Indians, on the other hand, as compared with those between Negroes and either the one or the other, are insignificant.

What are some of these differences in physical form? The lips of the Negro are thick; those of the European and Indian are thin. The nostrils of the Negro are broad, while the nostrils of the Whites and Indians are narrow. The legs of the Africans are long in proportion to their total stature; that is, their height sitting is short as compared with that of the other two racial groups. Skin color is the outstanding trait which exhibits difference, while other traits, such as finger-length, interpupillary distance, stature, hip width, etc., show characteristic statistical differences between the races.

As a control, therefore, I employed a series of 538 adult males, measured partly in New York City, but mainly at Howard University. I left them in the eight-fold genealogical classification I have mentioned above, and then tabulated the statistical constants—the averages and variabilities—for the several classes. It is the averages which are of importance in considering the validity of the genealogies, although I give the variabilities as a matter of procedure, and for the reason that I shall refer to them in a later chapter. It is apparent that, if the genealogies given me were actual statements of fact, and if the amount of crossing has any proportionate effect on bodily form, there should be fairly definite results. There should be differences between the averages for the several groups; in any given trait the unmixed Negro class should be very near the average for the West African populations; the group more Negro than White should be somewhat less like the African and tend more toward the White norms; and so on, until we reach the group claiming to be more White than Negro, which should be nearest of all to the White averages. I have intentionally omitted mention of the Indian mixture, and for two reasons. In the first place, I rather doubt whether there was enough Indian blood in any given family to make a perceptible difference, although one sees Negroes from time to time with strong Indian cast of features. The other point is more serious, from a biometric aspect, for the only

The Amalgam He Represents

trait in which Indians and Whites are unlike (this difference being always understood as relative, to the extent to which both differ from Africans) is in the breadth of the cheek-bones. And it so happens that in this particular trait, Negroes and Indians resemble each other. Therefore I consider here only the classes with different amounts of Negro-White ancestry, and I do not give the Indian-mixed classes, which in general follow the corresponding groups without Indian blood.

Let us now check our genealogies with physical measurements. First of all, we shall consider nostril width, the Negro nose being broad, the White nose narrow. When we express this width in millimeters what do we find?

Genealogical Class	No. of Cases	Average	Variability (σ)
Unmixed Negro	109	43.4	2.8
More Negro than White	129	41.35	3.4
Same amount of Negro and White	95	39.9	3.0
More White than Negro	30	37.5	3.9

This is striking evidence, but it is not enough. It is axiomatic in the best biometric practice of today that many traits must be utilized in the analysis of human groups. Therefore let us next take height

The American Negro

sitting, in which, as I have said, Whites are taller than Negroes. These results, in centimeters, are:

Genealogical Class	Average	Variability (σ)
Unmixed Negro	87.3	3.1
More Negro than White	88.1	3.3
Same amount of Negro and White	88.35	3.3
More White than Negro	89.1	3.2

Again the trend is what would be expected were the genealogies valid. But let us take a third trait, this time the thin White as against the thick Negro lips. Expressing the averages in millimeters, we find:

Genealogical Class	Average	Variability (σ)
Unmixed Negro	23.9	4.2
More Negro than White	22.5	4.3
Same amount of Negro and White	22.0	3.9
More White than Negro	18.8	3.8

Again this checks. But before we assert our conviction that the genealogical statements of these individuals are valid, let us take the outstanding test, that of skin color. It so happens that the use of a color top gives a quantitative expression of darkness. By mixing black, red, white, and yellow, the color of any skin can be matched. If we tabulate the percentages represented by the black segment of

The Amalgam He Represents

the surface of the top for the cases studied, we shall have an expression of relative darkness that can be handled statistically. The higher the percentage, the darker the individual or the average of the group. What do we find when the percentages of the individuals making up these genealogical classes are tabulated? The result again is striking:

Genealogical Class	Average	Variability (σ)
Unmixed Negro	75.5	10.3
More Negro than White	68.3	11.6
Same amount of Negro and White	61.2	12.0
More White than Negro	48.7	13.7

That is, the unmixed Negroes are markedly darker, on the average, than the other genealogical groups, while the class whose members told me that they represented more White than Negro ancestry are, on the average, by far the lightest.

These figures, I think, show with reasonable conclusiveness that these Negro genealogies are statements of fact and may be used to represent the proportion of mixture at least in this particular group. Whether this group is representative of the American Negro population as a whole, is another problem, and one with which I shall have to deal later. Certainly many students might insist that I had no right to base generalizations on the study of groups which, they would claim, were the product of social selection. I hope to be able to show that the differences between the various parts of the Negro population are much less pronounced than is generally assumed *a priori,* and thus to answer these critics in advance; but for the present I am content if the reader will agree with me that, for the particular group under consideration, the physical check on the validity of the genealogical material is impressive.

It will be apparent that this information forces us to revise our conception of the ancestral background of the American Negro and our judgment of his ability to give us this ancestral background accurately. Since the time when the Dutch "man of warre" landed the twenty-four unfortunate "Negars" on the Virginia coast, millions of their fellows have been brought here. These have mingled with the Whites to an enormous extent, though not, popular impressions to the contrary notwithstanding, in the recent past—a point which I shall discuss later. They have also mingled with the American Indians on a scale hitherto unrealized. A mixture of all races—African, Caucasian, Mongoloid —the American Negro truly presents a fascinating example of racial crossing.

Our next step is to examine the resulting mixture, in order that we may see what this extraordinary and unsuspecting melting pot has brought forth.

The Amalgam He Represents

We speak of Negroes in this country, but plainly this is nonsense if we are employing the word "Negro" in its biological sense. The American Negro is an amalgam, and the application of the term "Negro" to him is purely sociological. But the phrase "American Negro" has real biological significance, and I shall attempt next to show that a physical type has developed from the mixture represented in his person.

II

The Physical Type He Is Forming

For the past two or three years we have been hearing about the "New Negro," and we have come to associate the phrase with the literary and artistic naissance taking place among a group of young Negroes in this country. The movement has been of no little social significance, for it means that the American Negroes—or, in any event, a small group of them—are claiming a portion of their heritage as Americans, and are identifying themselves more and more closely with the culture of this country which is theirs by birth. It is worth noting that this phenomenon has manifested itself only in recent years, only, in fact, since the Negro has consolidated his position in this country and thus made possible the leisure necessary for such a group. And it is both interesting and significant that it is just at the same time when we are discovering that the New Negro is with us in physical form as well as in spiritual achievement, that a New Negro has indeed come into being, and that he is the American Negro.

The Physical Type He Is Forming

I do not intimate, of course, that there is any causal relationship between these two phenomena. It is a matter of coincidence, interesting though it be; for it must be evident that while achievement in culture waits until opportunities are opened to an oppressed people, the development of distinct physical form is a matter of generations. Moreover, this is particularly true of a highly mixed stock such as we find in the American Negro. As has been shown, there are in his ancestry all of the principal racial elements of which humanity is composed—White, Negro, and Mongoloid. And from this mixture there is being welded, and is already discernible, a definite physical type which may be called the American Negro. It is not like any type from which it has come; it is not White; it is not Negro; it is not Mongoloid. It is all of them, and none of them.

Such statements as I have just made contradict accepted views so completely that the point must be thoroughly demonstrated before it will be believed. As we look at the American Negroes we see about us everywhere, we behold men and women exhibiting such varieties of color, of racial cast, of stature and of build that it becomes difficult to grasp how all these traits may be associated with a definite physical type. Can it be that all these individuals are to be classed together? They range from the man of dark-brown skin and African appearance to the man who is

The American Negro

almost white, and from the broad-nosed, thick-lipped black man to the Caucasoid-looking, thin-lipped, narrow-nosed "technical" Negro. Then there is hair form, varying from the tightly curled to that of Indian-like straightness. Can these be grouped so that we may maintain that they constitute a definite physical type? It seems almost incredible. But before we pass judgment, let us recall the differences that are to be found in any so-called "pure" stock. In the White population of this country we find variations in eye-color, in hair-form and color, and certainly in those physical traits which can be measured, that equal and probably surpass the range of variation found among the Negroes. One trait in all likelihood furnishes an exception to this statement, and it is precisely this trait, curiously enough, that makes it so hard to believe the validity of the assertion which I have made. The trait is skin color. The pigmentation of Whites has never been studied by the method which I have employed in the study of the American Negro, but I believe that the skin color of Negroes, even unmixed African Negroes, is more variable than that of Whites. And it is pigmentation we first think of when the physical type of Negroes is being discussed, and in too many cases it is the only trait that comes to our minds. This is quite natural, because it is the most apparent trait. But if we think in terms of lip thickness, stature, head-

The Physical Type He Is Forming

form, and all the other thirty traits that have been measured in the course of this study, we will not be quite so certain.

What do we mean when we speak of a type? We must first introduce the idea of a variable. If one measures any natural phenomenon, one finds that there is variation in the thing measured, and that if one has a large enough number of cases they will distribute themselves about an average value in a manner that is well understood by statisticians and is termed the "normal" or "Gaussian" distribution. Now, in dealing with human populations, one finds that while they usually follow the rule which applies to other natural phenomena, there is a difference in the extent to which individual groups vary about their central or average values. Some spread more widely than others, or, to put it technically, the variability of one population is greater than that of another. It must follow, then, that when many traits of a population show a low variability, that population may be spoken of as homogeneous, or, as I have phrased it here, as constituting a "type." This, therefore, is what I mean when I say that the American Negroes are forming a definite physical type. In trait after trait, if one measures them and computes their variabilities, and if one then compares these with the variability in the same traits of unmixed African, European, or American Indian

The American Negro

populations, one will find that in most of the traits measured the variability of the greatly mixed American Negroes I have measured is as low as, or lower than, that of the unmixed populations from which it has been derived.

Let us see how this works out. If we consider the total height of the face, for example, we find the following variabilities for certain populations that have been studied:

Number of cases	Population	Variability (in mm.)
2,384	English criminals	7.70
72	Kagoro (West Africa)	7.52
20	Ekoi (West Africa)	6.82
247	Old Americans (White)	6.72
537	Pure Sioux Indians	6.37
534	*Mixed American Negroes*	*6.31*
40	Vai (West Africa)	5.84

Here we see that the variability of the American Negroes (represented by a series of male Negroes from Howard University, the typicalness of which will be discussed later) is very low. Indeed, only the sample of a West African tribe, which presumably represents much less mixture than is characteristic of our American Negroes, has a lower variability. The other populations mentioned, including other West African peoples, are all more variable.

The Physical Type He Is Forming

Suppose we now consider the height of the ear, a trait which very noticeably sets apart Negroes, on the one hand, and Whites and Indians, on the other. In the former the ear is small and fine, while in the latter two races it is large. Here, then, we have a distinctive trait for purposes of comparison:

Number of cases	Population	Variability (in mm.)
84	Marquesan Islanders	5.72
247	Old Americans (White)	5.72
2,338	English Criminals	4.88
959	*Mixed American Negroes*	*4.32*
20	Ekoi (West Africa)	3.96

The figure indicating the low variability of these American Negroes in this trait is striking, particularly when compared with the figure for inbred Old American Whites measured by Dr. Hrdlička.

If we take height sitting as another example, for the variabilities of various populations we get the following (in centimeters):

Number of cases	Population	Variability
30	Kajiji (West Africa)	3.94
96,239	White American troops	3.51
539	Pure Sioux Indians	3.50
897	*Mixed American Negroes*	*3.45*
19	Ekoi (West Africa)	3.07
37	Kagoro (West Africa)	3.00

The American Negro

Here again we find that the mixed American Negroes are comparatively low in the scale of variabilities, and we note especially that they are lower than the large series of White soldiers measured by Dr. Davenport and Dr. Love during the recent war. We find the same relative variability in the figures which Professor Todd of Western Reserve University obtained after a study of one hundred cadavera of Whites and one hundred cadavera of Negroes. These cadavera were those of paupers, and therefore represented a certain economic selection; but the comparative variabilities are nevertheless of interest, that for the White cadavera being 3.41 centimeters, and that for the Negro 3.19 centimeters.

I might go on and quote trait after trait, giving the variabilities for many more populations than I have cited above, were it necessary. The same low comparative variability for American Negroes has been noted by other students. For example, in a very recent paper William F. Ossenfort, working on skeletal material at Washington University in St. Louis, found the atlas, or first vertebral bone, of Whites to be more variable than that of his American Negro sample. Of course, variabilities are themselves variable, and they would change slightly one way or another with different samples of the same population. Nor does the rule of low variability

The Physical Type He Is Forming

always hold for the American Negro sample. Thus, for instance, if we consider the cephalic index, the trait beloved of the physical anthropologist, we find the American Negroes have a relatively high variability:

Number of cases	Population	Variability (in mm.)
167	Western Reserve Univ. White Skulls	4.74
126	Delaware Indians	3.50
961	*Mixed American Negroes*	*3.45*
19	Ekoi (West Africa)	3.27
55	Kajiji (West Africa)	3.07
727	Old Americans (White)	3.01
40	Vai (West Africa)	2.96

But even here, although my sample is more variable than the highly selected series of Old Americans, it is less variable than the skulls of Western Reserve White paupers, or of a series of Delaware Indians. And the high variability of this trait is all the more interesting, since in head-form there are only slight average differences between northern Europeans and Africans and eastern American Indians.

There is considerable evidence, therefore, that the American Negroes have gone far in creating a distinct type of human being. As I have said, the

The American Negro

rule of low variability does not always hold. All in all, I measured thirty traits in the course of this study. For twenty-three of them I found sufficient information regarding other populations to serve as a basis for comparison. In ten of these the American Negro series is high on the list, *i.e.,* shows high variability; in six it is at or near the bottom; and in the other seven it is at about the center of the list. This is striking evidence of the validity of our assertion that a type is being established.

There is another consideration that should be introduced here. Studies of population types and racial differences often neglect the important fact that human beings are found in related groups which we call families, and which in the aspect of descent may be called family lines. The variability of any population is made up of two parts, that of these family lines, and that which remains, *i.e.,* the variability within the families. Taken together, these two must account for the entire variability of the population. It is obvious that a people among whom a great deal of inbreeding has occurred will have a very low variability of family lines, because, since there has been this inbreeding, the ancestry of each of the families must be about the same as that of every other family. On the other hand, in a population where there is free mixture between all types, the variability of the families would be large, for

The Physical Type He Is Forming

one ancestral strain might be north European, another Slavic, another Italian, and so on. Therefore, the computation of the variability of the family lines in a population gives an excellent idea of the extent to which that population is homogeneous or heterogeneous. The variability within the families is also of importance. If we have a population which is inbred and which has originally come from a homogeneous stock—a population such as the Tennessee mountaineers, where there has been inbreeding, but where the original ancestry was unmixed English—both the variability of the family lines and the variability within the families would be low. But if we find an inbred population which originally came from very different types, then while the variability of the family lines might be low, that within the families would be relatively high.

To compute the variability of the families in a population and that within such families, it is necessary to have a large number of sets of brothers and sisters, or fraternities, as I shall call them. These requisite data were obtained when I measured a considerable number of children in one of the New York Public Schools in Harlem, where there were many such fraternities. From these data I computed these two variabilities for the cephalic index, as it is for this trait only that comparative material is available. The results were as follows:

The American Negro

Population	Variability of Family Lines	Variability within Families
Potenza, Italy	2.41	2.52
Central Italians	2.39	2.72
Bohemians	2.37	2.61
Worcester, Mass.	2.36	2.36
East European Jews	2.29	2.52
Scottish	2.17	2.66
New York mixed Negroes	*1.85*	*2.93*
Blue Ridge Mountaineers	1.85	2.09
Chippewa Indians	1.77	3.32
Mississaugua Chippewa	1.47	3.10
Bastaards (South Africa)	1.26	2.52

The low variability of the American Negro family lines, as revealed in the computations, was entirely unexpected. Hence I carefully checked them before I would accept the result, for this was before I had the data which showed the general lowness of variability already discussed. To find that a mixed New York Negro population, which included persons born not only in the United States but in the West Indian Islands as well, had the same variability of family lines as the inbred Blue Ridge mountaineers measured by Dr. Isabel Carter, was most astonishing. For the other populations the figures are reasonable enough. The inhabitants of Worcester represent groups from all parts of Europe, so that we should expect high variability

The Physical Type He Is Forming

of family lines. So also with the others. The central Italians represent a mixture in this trait between the long-headed southerners and the short-headed northerners. Even the Bastaards, a tribe of South Africa, were understandable; for although they represent a mixture of Boers and Hottentots, the genealogies of their families, obtained by Professor Eugen Fischer, showed the great amount of inbreeding that was represented after the original crossing had occurred. But inbreeding, in the way that it occurs in a small isolated community, or in the population of a remote mountain valley, is not the sort of thing which has been occurring among our American Negroes.

The figures for the variability within the families reassured me in my first doubt, for it will be noted that variation within these families of American Negroes is, with only two exceptions, the highest for all the populations listed. Professor Boas suggests in his discussion of the high figures for the two Chippewa tribes—the exceptions to which I have reference—this is probably due to the fact that White ancestry may have been much more prevalent than these Indians themselves realized. Certainly a high variability within the families is what would be expected if we had the phenomenon of an original mixture of stocks that were greatly different—as different as White and Indian and Negro. It was

The American Negro

not until later, when the genealogical data from all of the American Negro population studied in this research were in hand, that I realized how accurate a picture the high figure for the variability within the families provided.

The inbreeding which the American Negroes are practising differs only in degree from that of a geographically isolated group. True, it is inbreeding on a large scale, but within a population which is socially isolated, and it is inbreeding which, through a compensatory mechanism, if you will, or through a recent growth of "race consciousness" that is evident to all who have dealings with the American Negro people, is being enforced within the group as well as upon it. The genealogical material I gathered told a story which seemed further to substantiate the hypothesis of the development of a distinct type of American Negro through progressive lessening of intermixture with the White and Indian population. Although only about two per cent of the present college generation knew of White parentage, about ten per cent knew of White grand-parents, and those who knew their ancestry farther back reported even a larger proportion. The pressure within the Negro community, as well as that of the larger community of which it forms a part, against sexual relations between Negroes and Whites, is of great importance in this connection. I do not mean,

The Physical Type He Is Forming

of course, that there is a complete cessation of such mixture; for it seems unlikely that this will ever come about, no matter how strong the social disapprobation may become. But I believe that the amount of crossing at present is negligible in comparison with what it was in the time of slavery and shortly thereafter, and I further believe that these results point to such a conclusion.

It might be argued that my work was done among university and normal school students, in families which were firmly established both in the city and in the country, and that in such groups one would expect more rigid standards and fewer inter-racial meetings. But if we consult Dr. Ruth Reed's study of the unmarried mother in Harlem, we find that in five hundred cases of illegitimate birth among Negro women, only eight of the fathers were White men. I have talked to a large number of Southerners who might be expected to know the amount of racial crossing in the South, and they agree that the amount of illicit relationship, with resulting primary crosses, is amazingly small, although it is certainly larger than Dr. Reed found to be the case in New York.

Finally, to return to the table of variabilities of the family lines and the variabilities within these families, there is still further confirmation of the result discussed above. It may be remembered that I said that cephalic index, on the average, was about

The American Negro

the same in the crossed groups, African, north European and eastern American Indian. I decided to calculate the variabilities for the same fraternities for traits in which there is a known difference between these groups—interpupillary distance, nose width, height of ear, and length of middle finger (Negro hands, on the average, being longer and larger than White ones). The results follow:

Trait	Variability of Family Lines	Variability within Families
Interpupillary Distance	1.76	2.35
Width of Nostrils	1.81	2.10
Height of Ear	2.51	2.88
Length of Middle Finger	2.81	4.87

Here is confirmation of the results obtained when cephalic index was used, for in every case the variability of the family lines is distinctly smaller than that within the families.

Thus we have the phenomenon of a physical type in process of formation, as it were, before our very eyes. Both the lowness of the variability and the uniformness of the family lines contribute toward the substantiation of the hypothesis which was advanced at the beginning of this chapter, namely, that the American Negro is forming a distinct type of human being. The presentation is not complete, of course, for there are questions which must arise.

The Physical Type He Is Forming

One of them concerns the nature and description of this type, and another involves the manner in which the type was formed. Both of these I shall consider later. From the foregoing presentation, however, this much must be clear: that from as diverse racial stocks as it is humanly possible to assemble—Caucasian, Negro and Mongoloid—has come a type which is homogeneous and little variable—a veritable New Negro, the American Negro.

III

The Description of His Physical Type

THUS far in our discussion of the American Negro two prominent facts emerge: first, our historical knowledge of the Negro's racial past, together with the genealogical information I was able to gather and to substantiate by the use of physical measurements, indicate that he is a compound of the most diverse racial stocks; second, these measurements disclose a variability that is unexpectedly low for so mixed a population. These two facts are surprising, but both are well supported. Furthermore, we have the results of investigation of the family lines of the American Negro. These family lines were found to show a low comparative variability, indicating that this population is amazingly homogeneous. And since we have defined a type as a homogeneous population group, we must conclude that the American Negro is establishing (if he has not already actually established) a physical type that is as little variable as any of the unmixed parent stocks from which he has sprung. And we must further conclude that this homogeneity is the result

The Description of His Physical Type

of a sharp decrease in the amount of crossing between Whites and Negroes in this country, a decrease caused by the strengthening of the disapprobation with which the Negro community, now at one with the White in its attitude, regards such crossing.

If this is the case, then, two questions at once suggest themselves. First, since I have argued that there is a definite type in process of formation, how is this type to be described when compared with other peoples of the earth, particularly those from which the American Negro has come? To what extent is this type like the parent racial stocks? What light does the description of this type throw on the position of the school of biological thought which would insist that mixed offspring must resemble one of two parental types more than the other?

The second question, which also is fundamental to the argument I have presented, concerns the extent to which this type is representative of the entire American Negro population. In other words, how far may the Howard University and Harlem populations, the groups principally utilized in this study thus far, be said to represent the American Negro? It is repeatedly stated that there has been a very rigid selection of physical form which takes certain types for university students. Can the contrary be maintained? Is it not true, as is often asserted, that it is the more aggressive Negro who leaves the South and goes to Harlem? Is not the homogeneous physical type measured in this study the result of a special selection, and is it not wrong to assume that it represents the American Negro population?

These questions are entirely to the point, and are those which would first be asked by the skeptical expert in the field of biometrics. It is with the second, however, that we shall begin; for obviously, unless it can be shown that the sample is indeed representative, and that it is not composed of elements which themselves are the result of a social selective process which has taken certain types from the entire American Negro population, it will be pointless to describe the type. Indeed, unless the representativeness is clearly established, it would be fallacious to maintain that such a type is in process of being established by any but just those groups which have been measured.

We find ourselves facing a complicated problem, and we must exercise caution in our attempt to solve it. Social selection is a difficult thing to lay one's finger upon, and almost nothing is known about its operation. We surmise that cities, various industries, colleges, and the like, exercise a certain selection; and that there is such a selection from strictly economic and social groups, cannot for a

The Description of His Physical Type

moment be denied. By way of illustration, it is obvious that children of the well-to-do are more likely to go to college than are the children of the very poor. There may even be a selection of certain kinds of mental disposition. It has been maintained, for example, that the hardships of frontier life exerted a selective influence on the types of Europeans who came to America in the early days. And it is quite possible that the more adventurous and the more care-free did answer the call of the new country, leaving the timid stay-at-homes to work out their own destinies—and to hand on their timidity to their children. Similarly, it is more than possible that it is the adventurous Negro who answers the call of the northern cities. But the real difficulty is to connect this social or dispositional selection that acts upon physical build, ancestral stock, and racial characteristics, and this has never been done to the satisfaction of critical thinkers in the field of biometrics. Ammon, it is true, argued that there was a *natural* selection which brought the long-headed Bavarians to the cities, but it is quite possible that the difference in head-form between the city-dwellers and the people of the surrounding country may be due to the changed environment of city life. This possibility was indicated by Professor Boas in his study of the children of immigrants to this country, in the course of which he found that

The American Negro

children born in New York City exhibited a changed head-form when compared with their brothers and sisters who were born abroad.

I am not concerned, then, to deny the possibility that the groups studied may have been specially selected by the action of temperament and of social forces, but I do wish to point out that the connection between dispositional selection and the selection of physical form has never been proved. What I shall try to do is to show that the sample which I have used is, so far as physical characteristics are concerned, representative of the entire American Negro population.

The sample which I shall use here is the adult male series which has been available for this research. The entire series, including males and females of all ages, numbers almost 6,000 individuals. But here there are the factors of growth and of sex differences to be contended with. If we pick out the adult males in the series, we have a group of something under 900 persons for some traits, almost 1,000 for others, and from about 500 to 600 for still others. The differences in the numbers of cases result from the fact that not all of the thirty traits were measured on all the series composing the entire group. For when it was found, after a preliminary analysis of the results, that certain traits were not of great significance for the problem in hand, such

The Description of His Physical Type

traits were dropped from the study. The wisest method is that which utilizes only such traits as throw light on the particular problem which is being studied. This is sounder than the method employed by the older anthropologists, who arbitrarily selected certain traits without reference to the particular population which was being studied, and, having carried through the analysis of these arbitrarily selected traits, drew conclusions from the results.

If we take this entire adult male series, then, and compute the averages and variabilities, we find, as explained above, that the individual measurements scatter about an average value. This scattering, called the variability, shows us actually the chance that a given measurement will be found for the trait being dealt with in this population. Now, if we have two series from the same population, and if we know that one of them is representative, we can compute the extent to which the other will also be representative by finding out whether the differences between the averages for these two series are really of significance, or whether they are the result of chance sampling of the same population. And if the latter is the case, we can say that if one series is representative, the other must also be representative.

Now, it so happens that during the recent war Dr. Davenport and Dr. Love supervised the measurement of a very large and representative series

The American Negro

of American Negro soldiers—more than 6,000 of them, from the deep South, from the North, and, indeed, from all parts of the country. Let us see how the series of this study compares with the larger and admittedly representative army series for the three traits measured by Davenport and Love which were also measured by me:

Series	No. of Cases	Average	Variability
Stature			
Davenport and Love	6,454	172.0 cm.	6.9
Herskovits	887	170.5 cm.	6.4
Difference between averages, and variability of this difference:		1.5 cm.	.25
Height Sitting			
Davenport and Love	6,433	87.35 cm.	3.5
Herskovits	840	87.67 cm.	3.5
Difference between averages, and variability of this difference:		.32 cm.	.13
Width of Hips			
Davenport and Love	6,354	284.2 mm.	23.5
Herskovits	476	285.1 mm.	18.3
Difference between averages, and variability of this difference:		.9 mm.	.89

The Description of His Physical Type

When we look at these figures, we see that the two series may be assumed to be only chance samples of the same general population. The difference between two of the three sets of averages is statistically without significance, as any one trained in statistics can see at a glance in the table above by comparing the differences with their variabilities (which I have given so that those who wish to do so may check my statement). In the case of the third trait, stature, where this does not hold, we know from numerous other studies that stature is especially susceptible to environmental changes. I need not dwell on the differences in the food and physical surroundings, and type of exercise of the Negro in the usual run of civilian life and that which prevailed in the army. One can very plausibly maintain that the explanation of the average difference between the two series in stature lies here.

We may also investigate the question of representativeness by seeing what evidence the sample itself contains. This series is made up of several component parts. Negroes were measured at Howard University, in the Harlem district of New York City, and in a rural community of West Virginia. The Harlem series came originally from all over the country, and so did the Howard University men. More than this, about half of the Harlem series is composed of individuals who were born in the West

The American Negro

Indian Islands. Hence we have here an excellent opportunity to see to what extent the averages for the component series are alike, in order to understand further just how far the series itself may be regarded as representative of the American Negro population. Incidentally, these comparisons also throw light on the extent to which social selection is operative in taking certain types of Negroes to the cities, leaving others for the country, and sending still other types to universities. Let us first consider lip thickness, for here we should see whether there are any diffrences which affect the more Negroid as against the less Negroid of the population in their selection of occupation and place to live:

Group	Number of Cases	Average	Variability
Howard University	475	22.1 mm.	4.4
Harlem (born in United States)	67	20.8 mm.	5.5
Harlem (born in West Indies)	58	22.7 mm.	4.8
West Virginia rural	91	20.0 mm.	4.2

Or let us consider nostril width:

Howard University	475	41.0 mm.	3.9
Harlem (born in United States)	67	41.3 mm.	3.1
Harlem (born in West Indies)	58	42.6 mm.	3.7
West Virginia rural	91	41.6 mm.	2.8

The Description of His Physical Type

This is seen to be chance sampling about the general average; in other words, we have here differences which may be disregarded, statistically. Of course, it is impossible to give tables for all the traits which were measured, but it may be said that there are no important differences between the groups in any of the traits. One point should be emphasized—the striking resemblance between the American-born and West Indian-born Negroes. This, too, is something other than would be expected, until we consider that the African and European stocks represented are about the same, and that often slaves were left in the islands for acclimatization before being brought to the mainland. We perceive, then, that the term "American Negro" may perhaps be applied, not only to the Negroes of the North American mainland, but also to those living in its southern islands, as well. Even in studying pigmentation, we find that about the same average color prevails for all of the groups, and this, of course is an outstanding point.

But it may be objected that the Far South is not represented in any of these series. So far as my tables are concerned, I can only answer that a large percentage of the individuals in them were born in the South. And further there is available material from the so-called "Black Belt" which substantiates the results obtained from comparing my component

The American Negro

series. Miss Beatrice Blackwood kindly permitted me to tabulate the large series of measurements which she has taken on women at Tuskegee Institute, in Alabama, and on two other groups of women in Nashville, Tennessee. The Tuskegee women come from families of all occupations, and represent quite adequately the southern Negro women. If we compare the averages of the adults of her series with the average for lip thickness and nostril width of the women who were measured in Harlem and in West Virginia, we find the following:

Group	Number of Cases	Average	Variability
Lip Thickness			
Tuskegee women	64	21.8 mm.	3.3
Harlem women (born in United States)	111	19.3 mm.	4.3
Harlem women (born in West Indies)	81	20.1 mm.	4.7
West Virginia women	124	18.5 mm.	4.1
Nostril Width			
Tuskegee women	64	37.2 mm.	2.9
Fisk University women	24	36.1 mm.	2.6
Nashville Normal School women	82	36.5 mm.	3.8
Harlem women (born in United States)	111	37.9 mm.	3.4

The Description of His Physical Type

Harlem women (born in West Indies)	79	38.3 mm.	3.0
West Virginia women	124	38.0 mm.	3.3

Once more we discover no important differences between these norms, and we conclude that the Negro type which is being established is real and definite, and that it may apparently be tapped for a sample in any locality with consistent results. A conscious selection, of course, may change the results, as happened with a series measured under my direction among the professional and well-to-do classes in Harlem. But our purpose in measuring such a series was to make it a selected one and hence not representative. The difference between this group and the general population of which it forms a part will be discussed in a later chapter. But for unselected groups, the averages and variabilities show a consistency surprising to anyone accustomed to think of the American Negro as segregated into geographical, occupational, and educational groups according to the presence or absence of Negroid traits.

Since we see that there actually is an American Negro type, and since it is clear that my assumption of its existence is not a generalization based on an unrepresentative selection, we must ask ourselves the relation of this type to its parental types. Let us take a number of traits, and compare the averages for

The American Negro

these traits in American Negroes with the averages for some of the African, American Indian, and northern European populations from which we can assume the American Negro population to be descended. Stature is an outstanding measurable character, and one which is more or less stable in human populations. The West Africans are, as a rule, short, while the eastern Indians and the northern Europeans are tall. What happens when we mix them? Englishmen from Cambridge average 174.9 centimeters; the Old White Americans, 174.3; Iroquois Indians, 172.7; and Scottish men, 172.1; while the White troops measured in the army during the last war averaged 171.97 centimeters. The entire adult male sample measured in this study averages 170.49 centimeters in stature. Let us now consider the Africans. The Kanuri-Bornu (and all these are from West Africa) average 171.0 centimeters; the Mandingo, 170.5; the Fan, 169.8; the Kajiji, 168.3; the Ekoi, 166.9.

Let us now consider height sitting, which in the true Negro is smaller than in the White. The White troops measured 90.4 centimeters, and the Indian troops, 90.1; as we have seen, the Negro troops measured 87.35, and my series of Negroes 87.66. What of the Africans? The Kagoro of West Africa average 86.51 centimeters; the Ekoi, 86.0; the Kajiji, 84.44. Again, let us take cephalic index, for,

The Description of His Physical Type

in spite of the closeness of the northern Europeans to West Africans in the shape of the head, the latter are a bit longer-headed than the former, while the eastern American Indians are round-headed. We find that the Iroquois have an average index of 79.3; Englishmen at Cambridge, 78.3; Old White Americans, 77.95. The American Negroes of this sample average 77.04, while the Africans, to quote only some of the tribes for which averages are available, are as follows: the Vai, 76.05; the Kagoro, 75.8; the Banyange of the Cameroons, 75.4; the Ekoi, 75.3.

I might go on for trait after trait and quote the comparative measurements of these American Negroes and other populations, but I shall take only one more trait, one which I have often used before, since it is such an excellent index of Negroid physical character, and one in which pure Negroes and pure Whites and Indians differ to a marked degree. This is nostril width. Unfortunately, we do not have this measurement for many European populations. However, Todd's White cadavera had noses averaging 35.0 millimeters, and a series of Armenians were found to average 37.2 millimeters. The pure Sioux average 39.9 millimeters, as against the Montagnais-Naskapi Indians of the Northeast, who average 37.6 millimeters. The American male Negro sample averages 40.8 millimeters. Again, we make a comparison

The American Negro

with the Africans. One West African tribe, the Vai, averages narrower nostrils, the figure being 38.25 millimeters; but the Ashanti average 42.5 millimeters, the Ekoi, 43.95; the Kagoro, 44.41; the Kajiji, 45.5.

To anyone reading these figures it should be clear that the American Negroes seem to have combined traits of the peoples from which they have come in such a way as to represent today a blend of these types. Two arguments support this conclusion. In the first place, if we take a series of populations presumably ancestral to the American Negro, and arrange them from highest to lowest according to the average measurements of the various traits to be considered, and if we then insert the American Negro norms in the proper places so that they are in order, we find that they fall between the Indian and European averages, on the one hand, and the African, on the other. Secondly, in blending these different kinds of lips, noses, and all the other physical features left them by their forefathers of these different races, the American Negroes have not increased their variability, but, as I have already shown, have consolidated these differences until they are as homogeneous as any of the populations from which they have come.

Now again the question arises: how is the American Negro type which is being established to be

The Description of His Physical Type

described? In the light of the averages which have been given, and of the fact that the American Negro averages used may be considered as typical of the American Negro population as a whole, I think that we are safe in saying that this type combines the traits of its ancestral racial types, and has so blended them that any given feature is about equidistant between the typical African feature, on the one hand, and the typical European and American Indian feature, on the other. We can therefore say, I think, that the American Negro resembles all of his ancestral types, and yet is none of them. He is distinctive among human beings. Varied though American Negroes may seem to our untrained eyes, when we actually test the extent of this variation, we find that it is no greater than that found among any of the so-called "pure races" from which they have come.

One word of caution is essential at this point. The phenomena which we are observing are not static. They are changing, and, like all things human, they are never entirely consistent. We find that the American Negro average does not always fall just between the African and Caucasian-Indian; for example, the American Negro is almost as thick-lipped as the African. But by and large our generalization holds. We found the same result when we compared the variability of American Negroes with that of other peoples. It was not always low, but in the majority of traits we found that it was. It should also be noted that this American Negro type will never be established, if the bars which prevent racial mixture are broken down, or if for any unforeseen reason there should be a large migration to this country of pure Africans who would mingle their blood with that of the American Negroes. Judgment of human types is always more or less a thing of the moment, a matter of weighing and balancing. But it is safe to say that the large weight of evidence favors the position which has been advanced here, and we may confidently state that the American Negro type is before us.

Yet there has been a mechanism which has caused its formation. Some sort of selective process must be operating to produce the type. As I have remarked, social selection is not an easy thing to discern. But I believe that the process which has made, and is making, for the establishment of the physical type of American Negro we have described can be segregated, and it is this mechanism of selection among American Negroes that must next be considered before we can be certain that the conclusions which have been put forth here are tenable.

IV

White Values for Colored Americans

THE student of race and of the differentiation population groups is often so intent on physical form and the measurement of minutiæ of anatomical structure that he overlooks the fact that man is not only a biological creature but also a social animal. Particularly in studies such as this, which reveal the formation of a distinct physical type almost before our very eyes, the fascination of working out the hereditary mechanisms involved and of recording the changes in form and structure is such as nearly to blind us to the exceedingly important fact that the American Negro, no less than his fellow humans throughout the world, has his social as well as his biological aspect.

Just what is the significance of this fact for our study? We have asserted that the American Negro is an amalgam formed of types of the principal human racial stocks; that he has consolidated these diverse elements which are found in his ancestry into a homogeneous physical type; and that this type is statistically describable as one lying about

The American Negro

half way between the characteristic features of the parent stocks. Nevertheless, scarcely a single fact has been mentioned that might be described as sociological, with perhaps one exception: it has been pointed out that the formation of his type has been encouraged by the extent to which the Negro community, as well as the White, frowns upon interracial matings. In this connection it was pointed out that, should the current attitude toward so-called "race crossing" change, it would have a fundamental effect on the conclusions which we have reached. Indeed, in a few years our arguments would be vitiated, since the introduction of this new stock would change the type, were the crossing general enough, so that it would no longer be recognizable.

Why is this point insisted upon? Obviously, if conditions change will there not be a corresponding change in the results? The hypothesis goes much deeper, however, for this question of attitudes toward intermarriage raises the larger and more difficult question of the way in which our dominantly White culture acts upon the Negro community. This problem has been studied scarcely at all. Yet if we wish to understand the way in which the American Negro type has been formed we must understand how the Negroes have adjusted themselves to this predominantly White civilization, and how that

White Values for Colored Americans

civilization has influenced the ways of action and thought of the Negro members.

Let us consider, for a moment, the way in which a social entity acts upon its members. Any society displays in given situations methods of thought and ways of behavior which are fundamental to that society, and which, ordinarily, differ more or less from the reactions to similar situations of the members of other societies. These reactions are learned so thoroughly and at such an early stage of existence that they are taken for granted, and usually a member of a society does not think of them as having been learned, but regards them as he does such instinctive reactions as blinking his eyelids to guard the eyes against a blow. There are all gradations of these learned reactions, from the very deep-seated ones which, as I have said, are learned so thoroughly that they seem inborn, to those which are quite conscious and even cost us an effort, such as conformity to a new style of dress which has recently come into fashion. Generally speaking, the culture patterns which come nearest to being unconscious carry with them deep emotional content, so that actions which do not conform with them arouse immediate and violent emotional reaction on the part of the individuals who live in the culture in which they are prevalent. Take the manner in which the ordinary man regards the behavior of the immi-

The American Negro

grants with whom he comes into contact. His reaction to their foreign customs is immediate, since he feels that the only way of conducting the business of life is in accordance with the unconscious patterns of behavior which he has acquired.

What has this to do with the American Negro? We can put it briefly. He is set apart by his color in a culture in which the predominant traditions are not his, and the members of the predominant population group, both in numbers and in influence are different from himself. At the same time he must solve the business of living in this culture which is not his own. How can he do it? He must learn to adjust himself to his cultural environment if he would survive, and although he may take the current *mores* with a grain of salt, and although the isolation caused by his different pigmentation may bring about the creation of special culture patterns within his own group, he will, by and large, succeed only in so far as he adapts himself to the patterns to the dominant culture. The extent to which the Negro has done just that in this country is, as I have said, understood but little and studied even less. It has been vaguely realized by some students who have observed that the Negroes whose physical form is nearest the physical form of the dominant White group have the greatest advantages in the Negro community of this country; but further analysis has

White Values for Colored Americans

not been attempted. And it is just this acculturation which I wish to discuss here, since this process has had a far-reaching effect, not alone on the attitudes, but indeed, as I shall show, on the physical form of the American Negro.

Perhaps the reason why this observation has never been made with the force which the data I shall give below justify, is because no such study of this type exists. Yet one cannot work long in a Negro community without realizing that there are certain social forces in operation which penetrate the depths of the soul of the people. Nor was it long before I began to notice the manner in which the Negroes whom I measured in Harlem reacted to the patterns of the culture in which they found themselves. It so happened that I was measuring the children in one of the New York Public Schools, as a preliminary to visiting the homes to obtain measurements of complete families. It was essential for me to know when the parents of these children might be found at home, and I would therefore ask each child what work his father did, when he was usually at home, and when his mother might best be found there. It must be understood that, contrary to the general belief, the Negroes of New York are not a rich group. Indeed, it may be said that, with certain exceptions, the families of these children were not far removed from the poverty line, and that consequently a large

The American Negro

percentage of the mothers worked. It was with surprise that I found myself phrasing in two ways the question regarding the time when the mother would be at home. After a child had told me the occupation of his father, I would ask either "Does your mother work?" or "What kind of work does your mother do?"

It so happens that the culture-pattern which concerns the economic relation of men and women in the marriage state is clearly recognized. Except among the lower economic strata and, let me say, the upper intellectual classes, the general pattern of our culture is that the husband provides the living for the family, while the wife stays at home, cares for the children if there are any, or otherwise busies herself about the home. Here I had a Negro population on the economic line between a comfortable living and poverty. Where better might the extent to which they react to the prevalent economic pattern be studied? I tabulated the occupations of the fathers and then saw how many of the wives worked. The results were of great interest. The wives of the small business men, professional men, foremen, minor officials in the government services, ministers, and the like, did not work at all. Less than half of the wives of Pullman porters, waiters, red-caps, carpenters, and men engaged in similar grades of work were gainfully employed. The number of work-

White Values for Colored Americans

ing wives of janitors, elevator men, long-shoremen, barbers, and chauffeurs, to name a few occupations, was equal to those who did not work—an understandable fact when we reflect how such jobs may vary in the amount of compensation they carry. But more wives of day-laborers, ordinary porters, factory hands, and the like worked than did not work, while the list of the occupations of the men all of whose wives worked was that which included those lowest paid. Here we have an example of the way in which these American Negroes have responded to the operation of one pattern of the culture in which they live. The number of children in the family apparently has nothing to do with the matter. If the husband earns enough to support his family, the behavior of the wife in all respects follows the prevailing customs, and it is only when the occupation of the husband is not sufficiently well paid that the wife goes to work.

Now this same responsiveness to the patterns of the dominant White civilization is to be seen in almost any aspect of the Negroes' lives. Harlem, the greatest center they have created, is to all intents and purposes an American community peopled by individuals who have an additional amount of pigmentation in their skins. We see this at every turn. One finds, for example, a certain "one-hundred percentism" among the White population. Exactly the

The American Negro

same phenomenon appears in Harlem, though a large proportion of the Negroes residing there have emigrated recently from the West Indian Islands, Panama, and Central America. Time and again, on asking a person where he was born, I would receive a proud reply that he was born in the United States, that he was not one of those foreigners. The American Negro is played upon by essentially the same cultural forces as the Whites, and even in an accentuated degree. And why should this not be? Let us imagine his situation. Because of his color he is penalized wherever he turns. He may not travel as he will, he may not eat where he wishes, he may not select the place where he wants to live, he often fails to secure the position he deserves, he may have difficulty in educating his children in the school of his selection, shopkeepers prey on him, and he must often pay a premium because his skin is darker than his fellow's—all of these factors shape his existence. The fact that he is a Negro is something which figures in his life every hour of the day, something he is never allowed to forget. Is it strange, then, that he should unconsciously glorify that which is like the traits of the group enjoying every opportunity that is denied him? Is it surprising that he should term Negroid hair and features, for example, "bad" and the less Negroid "good," and that the lighter colored, *i.e.,* those having the suggestive

White Values for Colored Americans

designations of "brown," "high-brown," "high-yellow," "ginger-brown," "fair," "fair-brown," "red," "pink," "cream-colored" and "bronze," should have the advantage in his community?

That the lighter colored Negro has an advantageous place among the Negroes themselves has been recognized. Sometimes it is ascribed to historical reasons and the acquiescence in the general culture-pattern that I have described. More often, however, it is attributed to the greater percentage of White blood in the lighter colored of the American Negro population. Now, of course, this may or may not be true, but I must confess that I am skeptical, particularly since those who make this claim usually also insist on the inferiority of the "mongrel" when compared with the full-blood. To test their claim, however, I availed myself of an opportunity to show statistically any relationship which might exist between Negroid traits, as representing the amount of mixture in an individual, and his standing in the intelligence tests which determined his fitness for a college career. The results showed that there was no relationship whatsoever. I have no doubt at all, however, that the non-Negroid-appearing Negro has an advantageous position in the Negro community for social and historical reasons. It manifests itself strikingly in many ways. Professor Reuter, for example, found that a very large percentage of Negro leaders

The American Negro

in every sphere were mixed-bloods. It may be, of course, that, since the entire Negro population is so much more mixed than has been generally thought to be the case, the chances of finding a Negro leader who was not mixed are very small. But it must be remembered also that the earliest freed slaves were those of mixed-blood, very often the light colored ones, and it is the descendants of these who have had the best chance to make their way in a civilization the standards of which are essentially White standards. Then, too, there are actual discriminations within the Negro population against its own darker members. I found to my astonishment that it is difficult for a dark college man to "make" a Negro Greek letter fraternity, while the social opportunities for the women who happen to have distinctly Negroid features and coloring are very small indeed. In fact, the popular men and women at Negro schools or in Negro circles generally are ones who are light in color, as their less fortunate fellows well realize. When I presented this proposition to a forum of Negroes I obtained in reply a spontaneous chorus of "That's so!" from the darker persons in the audience.

To test this hypothesis further, we undertook a special study—the measurement of a large number of families of the well-to-do and professional classes. We found very striking differences between the gen-

White Values for Colored Americans

eral Harlem series and this specially selected series, composed of men from families in favorable economic circumstances, men most of whom have led successful lives in their communities. Thus, for example, the average nostril width of the well-to-do Harlemites (males) is 37.5 millimeters, while that of the general population is 41.3; the average lip thickness of the former is 19.8 millimeters, that of the latter 20.8. In pigmentation we find that for the well-to-do group the average percentage of black in the color-top used for skin color valuations is 56.7 per cent, while that of the general population is 68.8 per cent. (The higher the percentage of black, as has been explained, the darker the color.) We find a similar result when we compare the genealogies of these individuals with those of the general population of which they form a part. While only 7 per cent of all the well-to-do who were measured knew of no mixtures, 26 per cent of the series which came from the general Harlem population declared themselves to be unmixed Negro. Or, again, 20 per cent of these well-to-do declared themselves to have more White than Negro ancestry, while only 12 per cent of the general Harlem sample classified themselves in this way. We see, then, that the theory checks at all points, that the lighter, less Negroid individuals seem to have the favored position in the Negro community. But here the fact must again be

The American Negro

emphasized that this is not due to any inherent faculty conferred by the larger percentage of White blood. It is rather the result of a general reaction to the dominant patterns of behavior, induced by the fact that the Negroes live in a White civilization, and that unconsciously they feel that the easiest road to cultural salvation lies in adhering as closely as possible to these dominant cultural patterns.

What, then, is the relation between the study of the physical type which is being established in this country and the data given above? What is the biological effect of the reaction of the Negro to the cultural patterns of our civilization in a manner similar to the reactions of all of its other members? Very often this reaction is heightened because of the color difference obtaining between this minority and the majority group. As a matter of fact, this response to the demand of the dominant pattern has a direct influence on the manner in which Negroes mate. That there is such a selective mating, I have not the slightest doubt; and neither have the Negroes, although they do not often talk to White persons about it. But even casual observation of Negro couples will reveal that usually a man accompanies a woman who is lighter in color than himself. With such a selection in mating, we have the key to the mechanism which makes for the establishment of the American Negro type.

White Values for Colored Americans

Let us see how it works. At Howard University, where I first perceived that this might be an important social factor for the study in which I was engaged, I asked each man I measured who was the lighter, his father or his mother. When I tabulated the three possible answers I found they arranged themselves in this way:

Father lighter	30.3%
About the same color	13.2%
Mother lighter	56.5%

This seemed to indicate a strong trend toward selection, particularly since the parents of these men at Howard University live in every part of the United States where Negroes are to be found. And why should there not be this selection if Negroes respond to the same kind of cultural conditioning as Whites, particularly when we consider the prestige carried by that which is non-Negroid? For, after all, what is the pattern in our culture with regard to marriage? Is it not true that the great majority of men want to marry women who will bring them prestige, while the great majority of women wish to marry men who will, as the saying goes, "take care of them"? And why should it be any different with Negroes? Why should not skin color offer the invidious element necessary to confer distinction on an individual? I believe that this is exactly the state of affairs.

The American Negro

No clearer illustration could be found than a remark made to me by a Negro woman whose family I was measuring. "Of course a man wants to marry a lighter woman," she said. "Doesn't he want his children to be lighter than he is, and doesn't he want to lift up the race?" The dark man with a wife of light color finds many social and economic doors opened which would otherwise be closed to him; his lighter wife brings him the prestige he desires. And if the lighter individual is the more desirable, is not the economic position of the lighter colored wife more secure under this arrangement?

At the same time, whether or not this explanation was valid, the percentages remained. But they had to be controlled, and this control was available when we measured a large number of families in Harlem—families of people who came from all parts of the country and from the West Indian Islands as well. And when the results of the actual skin color observations on husbands and wives were tabulated, the percentages were as follows:

Husband lighter	29.0%
About the same color	14.5%
Wife lighter	56.5%

This is a striking confirmation. The average proportion of black in the color-top was 72.5 per cent for the husbands and 67.7 per cent for the wives, a de-

White Values for Colored Americans

cisive difference showing how much lighter, on the average, the wives are than their husbands. And lest it be argued that there is here involved the phenomenon of a sex-linked characteristic, I may say that the average for all the men of the entire Harlem series is 69.5 per cent, while that for all the women is 69.8 per cent—results which have no statistical significance as far as difference is concerned.

Here, then, in the process of social selection of light women by dark men, we see the mechanism for the consolidation of the type which has been formed by the American Negro. What happens to the light men? They probably "pass" over into the White group. A study of the census data for 1920 made by Mr. Charles S. Johnson showed that while there were 1,018 men for every 1,000 women of the class "Negro"—the dark individuals—there were only 886 men for every 1,000 women of the "Mulatto" group—the light ones. And what happens to the dark woman? I must confess that I do not know. It may be that they become the wives in second marriages; I note a tendency, where the wife is older than her husband, to find her also darker than he is. Then there is another consideration, that this variable of color is not fixed and that the term "lighter woman" is also variable. A woman who is lighter than a very dark man may herself be dark indeed, while it is not easy for a very light man to find a

The American Negro

wife lighter than himself. But, on the whole, this selective process is going on actively, and if it continues it will tend to stabilize the Negro type more and more firmly. Of course, it will make this type somewhat more Negroid on the average than it is at present, since the offspring of the women will be darker than they, and the females (we may disregard the males in this consideration) will again be selected by men darker than themselves. But the type cannot revert to the African, because of the large amount of White and American Indian blood that it contains.

It now becomes apparent that social as well as biological factors are of the utmost importance in the consideration of the American Negro type which is being established in this country, and which, it seems probable, will be more firmly established as time goes on, if there is no change in the attitude of society at large and of the Negro toward race-crossing. That the American Negro has established this type, and that it is something distinct, I do not believe can be doubted. And the significance of this fact for the general theory of race and for the work of the geneticists and biometricians, I shall attempt to show in the following chapter.

V
His Significance for the Study of Race

WHAT is a race? It is a question often asked and too readily answered, for we use it with amazing looseness. Not only do we apply it to the larger divisions of mankind, but we also speak of races when we have reference to nations, linguistic stocks, or cultural groups. I know of no definition of race that is both clear-cut and adequate; and yet the question is fundamental to all discussions of the part the biological basis of society (or race, if you wish to make the two synonymous) is said to play in the formation and maintenance of the bewildering variety of cultures which man has devised, and which some students are fond of rating as "higher" and "lower." That the biological element in the make-up of the human being is very important, no one will deny; but just what its importance is, remains one of the great puzzles of the biological sciences.

In the foregoing discussions we have worked through the problem of what has happened to the physical form of one human group during the time it has been in this country. We have seen certain definite results come from the study of these people, and we have seen further that here, as in many cases involving human beings, the social as well as the biological element has, in the final analysis, been instrumental in determining these results. But what is the significance of this work for the study of race and for an understanding of the biological processes involved in racial development? It is to this problem that we shall now turn, for the findings obtained in the course of this study are such as to throw light on certain points which are basic to many of the hypotheses advanced concerning the nature and functioning of race.

The geneticists and biometricians who have studied the subject have come to lay great stress on the variability of a population as an indication of the extent to which it is a "pure" racial stock. That is, it is asumed that a low variability points toward purity of race, and that a high variability is the result of much crossing. One need only quote some recent statements on the subject to show how generally students in the field accept this view. Dr. W. E. Castle, in a recent paper, remarks that "as heterosis disappears, the populations of later generations will be intermediate in character, and probably more variable than either uncrossed race." Dr. Clark Wissler, when he considers the topic of variability, discussed in a recent book of his, says that "what we

His Significance for the Study of Race

have . . . in a population unit is a number of types of pure lines, thrown together, each with its own range of variability and these variabilities have a way of combining so as to increase the variability of the whole. . . . As is often said, the range of stature will be greater among mixed races. This is, in fact, a recognized law of biology." Again, there is a recent work by Professor Hankins entitled "The Racial Basis of Civilization." Dr. Hankins lays great stress on the importance of racial differences in the making of a civilization, and in the course of his argument he gives some attention to the phenomenon of variability. He believes that crossings —that is, crossings between the upper ranges of ability of various races—are the desiderata; and one of the reasons he gives for this belief is that crossing makes for an increased variability which will make the range of possibility for excellence larger than it would be were the types which had been crossed to remain unmixed.

My own feeling is that students have assumed too freely that the mixture of different racial groups necessarily results in high variability. As a matter of fact, most of our knowledge of what happens under racial crossing comes either from studies of animals, or from studies of human groups that have been made without sufficient statistical analysis. When low variability is made an index of racial purity, I believe that we have assumptions for which there is no justification whatever. Yet the theory of Mendelian heredity, with its insistence on the inheritance of unit characters, points directly to such a position. If there is mixture between populations of very different physical traits, that is, different racial groups, it would be expected that the offspring of such crosses would partake to a certain extent of the characteristics of each of the parental types, and that there would be either a blend or a dominance in the first filial generation, and then a segregating out of these traits in the following generations. For if one population with a given variability in a certain trait mingles with a second population differing greatly in the same trait, the mixture between the two must increase the variability of the resulting generations. Of course, if we define a pure race as a group in which there is found low variability, that is one thing; but I am speaking here of the assumptions which are implicit in the theories held by the geneticists. If a racial group is one which is marked by well-defined physical characteristics, then a group having only those characteristics must be less variable, if the Mendelian hypothesis is operative, than another group which has inherited both these characteristics and those of another racial type. Therefore, it is held that a "pure" popu-

His Significance for the Study of Race

lation is less variable, and conversely, that low variability indicates racial purity.

Certain of the conclusions of this study, taken together with other researches, offer a number of trenchant arguments against this sort of hypothesis. Let us consider once again from what stocks the American Negro type derives: that is, from northern Europeans, from many kinds of Africans, and from American Indians from all portions of the eastern seaboard of North America. Certainly there is nothing of racial purity to be noted in this group. And yet if the discussion of variability is remembered, it will be recalled that the variation of this greatly mixed type, in trait after trait which was measured, is as small as, or even smaller than, the variation of many of the so-called "pure" populations from which it has sprung. Nor is this the only result of this kind which has come from studies of racial mixture. For example, the Rehobother Bastaards of South Africa, already mentioned, were found by Professor Fischer to have a low variability, in spite of the fact that they were the result of Hottentot-Boer mixture. The late Dr. Louis Sullivan, who worked through Professor Boas' Souian material, found that in many traits the half-blood Sioux were less variable than their full-blood ancestry. Davenport and Love found the same thing to be true of the American Negro sample which

The American Negro

was measured by them during the late war when the variability of the Negro was seen to be smaller than that of the other racial stocks in a majority of traits measured. Professor Todd's dissecting-room population, to which I have previously referred, showed that the Negroes in numerous traits are less variable than the unmixed Whites.

These are not results which would follow the orthodox criteria of racial purity. Why should the half-blood Indian be less variable than the full-blood? Why should the Bastaard be less variable than his Dutch and Hottentot ancestry? Or why, finally, should these American Negroes, who are mixed of all three of the primary human types, have as low or lower variabilities in trait after trait as their ancestral stocks? These are some of the problems toward the solution of which the findings which have been set forth may have something to contribute.

It will be remembered that in stating that the American Negro has formed a definite type of human being, I discussed the variabilities of the group as a whole. But before this, in giving the genealogical background of the entire group, I gave the averages and variabilities of these genealogical classes in order to show how the different averages varied in the same way as did the amount of Negro ancestry when the African averages were used as

His Significance for the Study of Race

criteria. Now if the variability of these genealogical classes for all the traits measured be considered, there is something interesting to be seen. The reader will recall that one of these classes was composed of unmixed Negroes, while the others were arranged according to the various amounts of crossing with White and Indian stock they represented. If low variability were correlated with racial purity, then we would expect that in a majority of traits measured the unmixed Negro group would be the least variable of all genealogical classes. But we find nothing of the sort; for this group has the lowest variability in only three out of the thirty traits that were measured. Or we can apply another test. We can add the variabilities for all the thirty traits for each of the eight genealogical classes, this giving us eight sums, and then see how the totals of these sums range themselves. The lowest is not the unmixed Negro, but the group including those individuals who gave themselves as having more Negro than White blood, with Indian mixture in addition. And though the unmixed Negro class is next in lowness in the scale of the summated variabilities, it is almost identical in this respect with another class which represents large mixture. This again is not a result in keeping with the hypothesis that low variability is a correlate of racial purity.

We may then fairly pose the question: what is the

The American Negro

significance of low variability? Certainly the data represented in this study do not seem to justify its utilization as an index of racial purity. And yet has variability no significance for the study of race? The answer, I take it, must be sought in a consideration of the populations in which low variability is found. The American Negroes show low variability. So do the Tennessee mountaineers. So do the Bastaards, and the old White Americans measured by Dr. Hrdlička. Yet a chance sample of White Americans, such as was measured in the army, or by Professor Todd in his dissecting-room population, does not show it. The answer to be gained from a consideration of these populations appeals to me as fundamental for our concept of the term "race." We are forced to conclude, I believe, that the problem which presents itself is not to be thought of in terms of the races to which a given population may or may not belong; nor is the fundamental point the extent to which this population is mixed or pure, with regard to a particular race or races. On the contrary, we should determine the extent to which the population being studied may be considered as homogeneous or heterogeneous in type (type here meaning a large number of physical characteristics); we should discover the historical connections that have made it what it is; and we should analyze the manner in which it has developed, if we can do so by study of

His Significance for the Study of Race

the parental types from which it has sprung. In the past, it seems to me, anthropologists have been too prone to place a population more or less arbitrarily according to its average in one or two or three traits (usually one, and that one the form of the head, or cephalic index) and, on the basis of the result, to say that it belongs to such and such a race, unless outstandingly obvious characteristics which could not be disregarded stood in the way. So arbitrary a method of placing populations in racial categories seems to me to be obviously unsound when one considers the amount of mixture which all contemporary peoples represent. Of course, one may broadly catalog a population as belonging to one of the major human groups—as White, as Negroid, or as Mongoloid. But this is usually a more or less self-evident classification.

The American Negroes are, after all, a homogeneous population. They are also a greatly mixed group. How may one reconcile these two statements? It is not so difficult when one really considers the proposition from all angles. For is it not true that all human groups represent large amounts of mixture? This brings us back to the theory of race. Students have wondered at the number of varieties of human types, and have been unable to account for them. They have also been at a loss to account for the degree to which all the so-called "races" of man seem to shade from one type into another; with never the sharp lines of demarcation that are found when we divide one biological species from another. For here enters an important point that is rarely touched upon. Professor Hankins, for example, completely ignores it in his consideration of race. Almost the only students to recognize its existence at all are Professor Eugen Fischer and some of his colleagues in Germany, who have concerned themselves with the problem as related to its effects upon certain of the lower animals, and the applications of their method and results when applied to human beings. The point is this: man is probably the oldest domesticated animal. Such a point may appear to be beside the main argument, but, as we shall see immediately, it is of the greatest importance.

What are the criteria of domestication? They are four: a stable food supply, a restricted habitat, protection, and restricted breeding. Man, as Professor Boas has pointed out, assured himself to a greater or less extent of these four when he discovered the use of fire. And certainly he assured such animals as became domesticated after him (or which domesticated themselves) of safety and food, and confined them in a more or less circumscribed locale. What have been the effects of all this on the wild forms? And how do domesticated animals differ from their fellows who are not domesticated? The important

His Significance for the Study of Race

point in our consideration of race is this: the domesticated animal is less stable than his wild brother. Physical forms which are unknown in the wild type appear, and these may even change with changes of food or of residence. If different types of domesticated forms are crossed they may be lost; for in such cases, we are told, wild types often reappear. At present some results of domestication are being studied in Philadelphia. Wild rats have been captured and bred in captivity, and they are still being bred and domesticated. The results show a change in physical form with each succeeding generation bred under the conditions of domestication—changes away from the wild type.

A change in physical form and a greater instability of type, then, seem to be the results of domestication. In the light of this fact, and also of the fact that man is the oldest of our domesticated animals, is it strange that we have all these varieties, and that there should often be large differences between children of the same families? The actual processes of heredity in man are seen as through a heavy veil which we have only begun to break. Most of our information as to how these processes work has been gained by inferences based on the study of the lower forms of life. Why should it not be that this incident in the racial history of man, his domestication, has been a deciding factor in the formation of the

The American Negro

numerous varieties of human beings we see in the world today? Why should it not be that the resulting added instability of type accounts for the fact that there are no sharp divisions between population groups? Why is it not possible that through the mixture of a number of types a new type may be formed, a type such as we have exemplified in the American Negro?

The objection will be immediately raised, I imagine, that our knowledge of the hereditary processes points to the inheritance of unit characteristics in the Mendelian ratio. That is, when two traits are crossed, there is observable a dominance of one over the other, the latter being termed recessive. In the first filial generation, that which follows the cross, according to the Mendelian law, the dominant trait alone will be apparent, but the recessive traits will again appear in a small proportion of offspring in the second and succeeding filial generations. Work along this line, with human beings, has been done particularly by the eugenists. Most of the traits in man for which they claim heredity in the Mendelian ratio are of a pathological nature, but their results, together with the striking work of Professor T. H. Morgan and his associates with the fruit-fly *drosophila melanogaster,* have convinced many that here we have a mechanism of the greatest importance in the consideration of population changes, and that

His Significance for the Study of Race

this provides the method needed to insure the perpetuation of the "best" types. Again, however, we may ask what light this study of the American Negro sheds on such a vexed problem? Can it be that, since we have worked with a human group which offers almost laboratory conditions in the study of population changes and race crossing—can it be that we will have here any confirmation of the hypothesis of Mendelian heredity which has been advanced so freely and so urgently? Let us see what our results have to contribute.

If we have a cross between two populations as different as Negro and White (for we may, I believe, disregard the Indian element here, since it was introduced into the Negro stock so long ago as to have been almost submerged in the larger flood of Negro and White blood of which it today forms a small portion), we should then expect one of the sets of traits to be dominant and the other recessive. But, the geneticist will say, this is much too crude. Each trait has its gene or set of genes, and while for one trait—skin color, let us say—the Negroid characteristic may be dominant, for another—lip thickness perhaps—the Negroid characteristic may be recessive. On the other hand, certain of these traits may be linked with others in the same chromosome, if not in the same gene, or there may be several genes controlling one trait, all of which might lead one

The American Negro

astray. But let us grant this readily, and go on with the argument. A given trait, let us say, is dominant in either its White or its Negroid aspect. Then, in the first filial generation, that of the primary crosses between the two types, the recessive trait would not appear at all—only the dominant, which, for the sake of argument, let us say, is wide nostrils as against narrow ones. But we need not concern ourselves with the primary cross, since the population we have considered is not the first or even the second filial generation, in the main, but is farther removed from the original crossing. Therefore, as a result of the subsequent sorting out of this unit character, lip thickness, in the mixed offspring which is our American Negro population, the statistical analysis of the resulting distribution of lip form would have to show two things. In the first place, the measurements should mass toward the dominant characteristics—toward the upper values, let us say, if the Negroid type were dominant, and should string out along the lower, or White values, and the average should be nearer the Negro averages than it is the White. But it will be remembered that this matter has been commented on at length in a preceding chapter, since this is just what is not found. What we see is that in trait after trait the average is about half-way between the averages for the White population and the African, so that what we have repre-

His Significance for the Study of Race

sented here is a blend, if the gross statistical analysis is correct. In the second place—and this I have said before—there would have to be an increase in variability if the Mendelian hypothesis were operative in this case. But I need not repeat the fact that the American Negro is homogeneous, and that the index of this homogeneity is the low variability of trait after trait when this variability is compared with that of the so-called "pure" populations.

Results such as these must give us pause. It may be that Mendelian heredity is operating in a way so complex that it cannot be discerned by the use of statistical analysis of adult groups, although this type of material constitutes by far the greatest portion of that available. When the actual heredity from parents to children is investigated, a new light may be thrown on the situation. But the data which have gone into this study of the American Negro thus far do not seem, when analyzed, to show any tendency to act according to the requirements of the Mendelian hypothesis.

And what of our good word "race"? Are we any nearer to an understanding of what it means? Only, I think, in a negative sense. If race means anything in the way of a definite physical type, then the American Negro is a racial group. If it means anything in the sense that lowness of variation is associated with racial purity, then the American Negro is a pure

The American Negro

racial group. But I do not claim the term "race" for the American Negro, and I certainly do not claim that there is anything but the most striking type of mixture represented in him. If anything, the theoretical significance of the work which has been presented in these discussions seems to be that it furnishes a dramatic illustration of how little we are able to define a word that has played such an important rôle in our political and social life, while it further illustrates how much we take for granted in the field of the genetic analysis of human populations.

The American Negro? Let us regard him as a homogeneous population group, more or less consciously consolidating and stabilizing the type of which he has commenced the formation. But let us not think of him as a new race, or as anything but the homogeneous group he constitutes. To do otherwise would be fallacious. And fallacious thinking, translated into action in the field of race, too often makes for tragedy.

Bibliographic Appendix

THE publications available concerning the Negro are countless. But there are very few treatments of the American Negro as an exemplar of racial crossing, and the study of his physical form is almost a virgin field. Most of the attention thus far given to him has concerned the more pressing economic and social problems of the day. This is only too well illustrated by a relatively complete bibliography recently published covering the study of the anatomy and anthropometry of the American Negro:

Aleš Hrdlička, Anthropology of the American Negro. Historical Notes and Bibliography. American Journal of Physical Anthropology, vol. x, (1927), pp. 205-235.

For the benefit of those who wish to go further into the problem of race-crossing, however, or who wish to have recourse to some of the papers on which I have based my own work in part, I append the following titles. The list does not pretend to be complete; it is presented merely to suggest leads to those who may care to follow them:

Franz Boas, The Half-Blood Indian, an Anthropometric Study. Popular Science Monthly, 1894.

—— ——, Report on an Anthropometric Investigation of the Population of the United States. Journal of the American Statistical Association, 1922, pp. 181-208.

Charles B. Davenport, Heredity of Skin-Color in Negro-White Crosses. Carnegie Institution of Washington. Washington, 1913.

Charles B. Davenport and Albert G. Love, The Medical

The American Negro

Department of the United States Army in the World War. Vol. xv, Statistics; part 1, Army Anthropology. Washington, 1921.

Eugen Fischer, Die Rehobother Bastards. Jena, 1923.

——— ———, Rasse und Rassenenstehung beim Menschen. Berlin, Verlag Ullstein, 1927.

T. Wingate Todd, Cranial Capacity and Linear Dimensions in White and Negro. American Journal Physical Anthropology, vol. vi (1923), pp. 97 ff.

T. Wingate Todd and Leona Van Gorder, The Quantitative Determination of Black Pigmentation in the Skin of the American Negro. Amer. Jour. Phys. Anthropology, vol. iv (1921), pp. 239-260.

(To these last two might be added numerous significant papers on Negro-White differences based on the important collections of American Negro and White skeletal and cadavera material available at the Anatomical Laboratory of Western Reserve University. Such of these papers by Professor Todd and his associates as pertain to the study of the American Negro data are named in Dr. Hrdlička's bibliography given above; others are to be found in the anatomical and anthropological journals.)

Clark Wissler, Distribution of Stature in the United States. Science Monthly, vol. xviii (1924), pp. 129-143.

Although we are not here directly concerned with the social and economic setting of the Negro problem in America, we are interested in the mechanism of acculturation to the social patterns of our civilization as it applies to the Negro. This acculturation lies at the root of the phenomenon of social selection which we found to be basic to the formation of the American Negro type. I mention only a few titles; the first is the best (indeed, the only adequate) discussion of the social situation of the Negro in America today; the next four treat some aspects of the process of acculturation;

Bibliographic Appendix

and the last throws additional light upon and tends to validate the findings set forth in Chapter IV as to the social selective process:

E. B. Reuter, The American Race Problem. New York, Crowell, 1927.

Guy B. Johnson, Newspaper Advertisements and Negro Culture. Journal of Social Forces, vol. iii (1924-1925), pp. 706-709.

Wallace Thurman, Negro Artists and the Negro. New Republic, vol. ii (1927), pp. 37-39.

G. A. Steward, The Black Girl Passes. Social Forces, vol. vi (1927-1928), pp. 99-103.

Eric M. von Hornbostel, American Negro Music. The International Review of Missions, vol. xv (1926), pp. 748 ff.

Charles S. Johnson, editorial in "Opportunity," The Vanishing Mulatto, vol. iii (1925), p. 291.

It would be impossible, in a book of this limited scope, to give in detail all of the data on which this study is based. That would entail the publication of material of a type which is useful only to the specialist (it will be published elsewhere). Only the results of my study, and the arguments on which it rests, have been given here. However, for purposes of allowing those who wish to check the statements made in this book, I give a list of some of the papers I have published dealing with this research. In these, the interested reader will find much more detailed and technical presentation of data, development of statistical formulæ, and elaborate discussion of method:

Some observations on the Growth of Colored Boys. Amer. Jour. Phys. Anthropology, vol. vii (1924) pp. 439-446.

Preliminary Observations in a Study of Negro-White Crossing. Opportunity, vol. iii (1925), pp. 69-74.

The American Negro

The Influence of Environment on a Racial Growth Curve. School and Society, vol. xxii (1925), pp. 86-88.

The Color Line. The American Mercury, vol. vi (1925), pp. 204-208.

On the Negro-White Population of New York City: The Use of the Variability of Family Strains as an Index of Heterogeneity or Homogeneity. Proceedings, xxi Congrès International des Americanistes. The Hague, 1924, pp. 5-12.

A Further Discussion of the Variability of Family Strains in the Negro-White Population of New York City. Jour. American Statistical Association, vol. xx (new series) (1925), pp. 380-389.

Social Pattern: a Methodological Study. Social Forces, vol. iv (1925), pp. 57-69.

The Negro's Americanism, in "The New Negro," edited by Alain Locke. New York, A. and C. Boni, 1925, pp. 353-360.

On the Relation between Negro-White Mixture and Standing in the Intelligence Tests. Pedagogical Seminary and Jour. of Genetic Psychology, vol. xxxiii (1926), pp. 30-42.

Correlation of Length and Breadth of Head in American Negroes. Amer. Jour. Physical Anthropology, vol. ix (1926), pp. 87-97.

Some Effects of Social Selection on the American Negro. Publications of the American Sociological Society, vol. xxxvii (1926), pp. 77-82.

Age Changes in Pigmentation of American Negroes. Amer. Jour. Phys. Anthropology, vol. ix, (1926), pp. 321-327.

Does the Negro Know His Father? A Study in Negro Genealogies. Opportunity, vol. iv (1926), pp. 306-310.

Social Selection in a Mixed Population. Proceedings of the American Academy of Sciences, vol. xii (1926), pp. 587-593.

Bibliographic Appendix

Growth of Interpupillary Distance in American Negroes. Am. Jour. Phys. Anthropology, vol. ix (1926), pp. 467-470.

Variability and Racial Mixture. The American Naturalist, vol. lxi (1927), pp. 68-81.

Some Physical Characteristics of the American Negro Population. Social Forces, vol. vi. (1927-28), pp. 93-98.

Index

American Indian,
  percentage of Negroes claiming partial descent from, 10
American Negro,
  See Negro, American
Amon, Otto, 37
Atlas,
  comparative variation of Negroes and Whites in, 24

Bastaards, Rehobother, 29, 71, 72, 74, 84
Blackwood, Beatrice, 44
Blending of ancestral types,
  as characteristic of American Negro, 48
Boas, Franz, 29, 37, 71, 76, 83

Carter, Isabel Gordon, 28
Castle, W. E., 68
Census, U. S. of 1920,
  sex ratios for mixed and unmixed Negroes, 65
  proportion of American Negroes representing mixture given by, 4
Cephalic Index,
  averages of for various populations, 47
  variabilities of various populations in, 25
Color terms used by American Negroes, 58 f.
Consistency of data,
  extent to which dependent on social facts, 50
Culture patterns,
  influence of dominant White ones on American Negro, 52, 54, 57, ff.
  nature and behavior of, 53

Davenport, C. B., 24, 39, 71, 83
Domestication,
  criteria of, 76
  importance of for study of race, 76 ff.
  results of, 77
Dowd, Jerome, 5
Drosophila Melanogaster, 78

Ear, height of,
  variabilities of various populations in, 23
Economic relation of man and woman,
  effect on American Negro of, 55 ff.

Facial height,
  variabilities of various populations in, 22
Families,
  variability within for various populations, 28
Family lines,
  significance of, 26 f.
  variability of in various populations, 28
Fischer, Eugen, 29, 71, 76, 84

Genealogical classification of Negroes,
  method employed in making, 8

Index

Genealogical method, objections to, 7
Genealogies of Negroes, reliability of, 8 ff.
validation of, 10 ff.

Hankins, F. H., 69, 76
Harlem (New York) series of American Negroes, 41
Height sitting,
 averages and variabilities of Negroes of various degrees of mixture in, 14
 comparative averages of for various populations, 46
 variabilities of various populations in, 23
Herskovits, Melville J., 85
Homogeneity,
 importance of in study of race, 74
Hornbostel, Eric M. von, 85
Howard University series of American Negroes, 12, 41
Hrdlička, Ales, 23, 74, 83

Inbreeding, significance of, 27

Johnson, Charles S., 65, 85
Johnson, Guy B., 85

Lip thickness,
 averages and variabilities of Negroes of various degrees of mixture in, 14
 comparison of component series of American Negroes in, 42, 44
Love, Albert G., 24, 39, 71, 83

Mecklin, J. H., 6
Man, as oldest domesticated animal, 77
Marriage,
 cultural pattern of in American society, 63
Mendelian heredity,
 significance of low variability for, 70
 simple, lack of confirmation of in this study, 79 ff.
Mendelian law,
 nature of processes of, 78
Morgan, T. H., 78
Mulatto,
 census figures for number of in 1920, 4
 social position and character attributed to, 5 ff.

Nashville, Tenn.,
 series of Negro women measured in, 44
Negro, American,
 applicability of term, 43
 census figures of 1920 regarding, 4
 comparative averages for various traits, 46, 47
 comparative variabilities for various traits, 22 ff.
 comparative variability of families of, 28
 comparative variability within families of, 28
 comparison of component series in various traits of, 42 ff.
 description of physical type of, 49
 inbreeding practised by, 30
 mixture with American Indians, 3
 non-negroid aspects of well-to-do, 61
 physical form of, 18 ff., 71
 racial ancestry of, 4
 regarded as homogeneous population group, 82
 results of genealogical classification of, 9
 selection in marriage on skin-color basis of, 63 f.
 soldiers measured and compared with series of this

[90]

Index

study, 40 f.
validity of genealogical statements of, 10 ff.
variability of and within families for various traits, 32

Negro,
biological and sociological significance of the term, 17
light colored, advantageous social position of, 59 ff.

"New Negro," the, 18

Nostril width,
averages and variabilities of Negroes of various degrees of mixture in, 13
averages of for various populations, 47 f.
comparison of component series of American Negroes in, 42, 44

Ossenfort, Wm. F., 24

Physical form,
differences between Negroes and Whites in, 11

Physical traits, consistency of averages of for various groups of American Negroes, 45

Physical types of American Negro,
homogeneity of, 32

Pigmentation,
as an non-sex-linked characteristic, 65
average and variability of Negroes of various degrees of mixture in, 15
comparative, of American Negro husbands and wives, 63 f.
quantitative method of determination of, 14 f.

Race,
lack of definition of, 67

significance of this study for definition of, 81 f.

Race-crossing,
as represented in American Negro, 16
extent to which found at present between Negroes and Whites, 31
phenomenon of, 3

Reed, Ruth, 31

Representativeness of American Negro sample used in study, 36 ff.

Reuter, E. B., 6, 59, 85

Sample of American Negroes used in study, size of, 38

Selection, social,
difficulty of determination of extent operative, 36
in marriage, of American Negroes, 63 f.

Social aspect of man,
in relation to biological aspect, 51

Stature,
comparative averages of for various populations, 46

Steward, G. A., 85

Sullivan, Louis, 71

Tennessee Mountaineers,
low variability of, 27, 74

Thurman, Wallace, 85

Todd, T. Wingate, 24, 72, 74, 84

Todd, T. Wingate and Leona Van Gorder, 84

Tuskegee Institute series of Negro women, 44

Type, physical, meaning of, 21, 74

Variability,
as an index of racial purity, 68 ff.

Index

Variability, comparative, of American Negro, 26, 71
Variability of family lines, significance of, 26 f.
Variability of genealogical classes of American Negroes, 13 ff., 72 ff.
Variability, significance of, 21 ff., 72 ff.

Western Reserve University, Negro and White cadavera from, 24, 72, 74
West Indian Islands, Negroes measured from, 41
West Virginia series of American Negroes, 41
Wissler, Clark, 68, 84